Cover and Title Page: Nathan Love

www.mheonline.com/readingwonders

Send all inquiries to:
McGraw-Hill Education
2 Penn Plaza
New York, NY 10121

ISBN: 978-0-02-131311-2
MHID: 0-02-131311-3

Printed in the United States of America

6 7 8 9 LMN 21 20

C

ELD
Companion Worktext

Program Authors

Diane August

Jana Echevarria

Josefina V. Tinajero

Mc
Graw
Hill
Education

FACT OR FICTION?

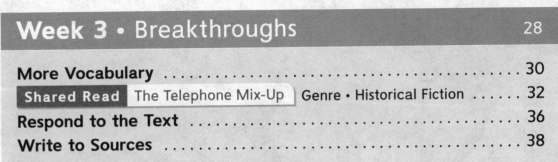

FACT OR FICTION?

THE BIG IDEA
How do different writers treat the same topic?

TALK ABOUT IT

Weekly Concept Our Government

? Essential Question

Why do we need government?

>> *Go Digital*

COLLABORATE

Look at the photo. Describe what you see. Discuss why people need government. Write words in the chart.

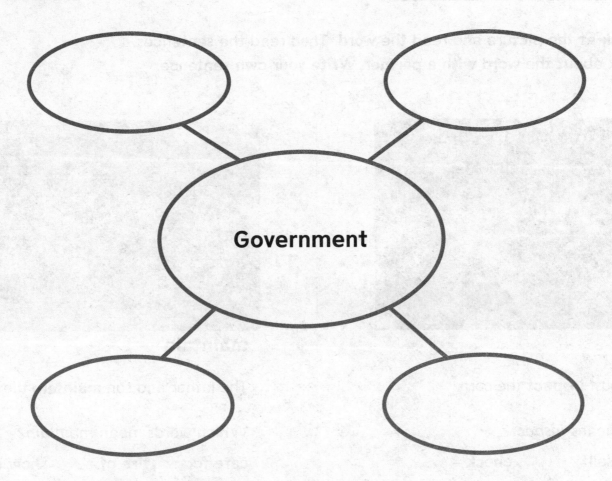

Government

Discuss why government is important. Use the words from the chart. You can say.

Government makes _____.

People need government because it helps to _____.

More Vocabulary

COLLABORATE Look at the picture and read the word. Then read the sentences. Talk about the word with a partner. Write your own sentence.

inspect

The farmer must **inspect** the corn.

What word means *inspect?*

buy   sell   check

Why do people inspect things?

People inspect things to _____

_____

_____.

maintain

The father and son **maintain** the garden.

Which words mean *maintain?*

care for   tire of   show up

What do you maintain?

I maintain my _____

_____

_____.

6

Words and Phrases: Preposition *by*

The word *by* can mean "go past."

Who does the boy run by?

The boy runs **by** the girl.

The word *by* can also mean "through the action of."

What did the trees get hit by?

The trees were hit **by** lightning.

COLLABORATE **Talk with a partner. Look at the pictures. Read the sentences. Underline the meaning of the preposition *by* that is used in each sentence.**

The diver swims **by** the coral.
    past   through

The forest was destroyed **by** fire.
    past   through

1 Talk About It

Look at the picture. Read the title. Discuss what you see. Use these words.

rules   school   playground

Write about what you see.

I see _____

_____.

Where is the girl?

The girl is _____

_____.

What is in the playground?

The playground has _____

_____.

Take notes as you read the text.

A WORLD WITHOUT RULES

CLOSED

Essential Question

Why do we need government?

Read how government and laws help to protect us every day.

8

Do you think rules stop you from having fun? What if we had no rules? Nobody would tell you what to do ever again! Let's see what it is like to live in a world without rules. You might not like it!

A Strange Morning

Let's start at home. Your alarm clock rings. There is no law that says you have to go to school. Since there are no rules, you can have cookies for breakfast! In this new world, you do not have to brush your teeth. But the next time you see the dentist, you may have a cavity.

A Community in Confusion

You don't have to go to school, so you decide to go to the playground. There is no crossing guard to help you cross the street. There are no traffic laws, so cars speed by. You don't want to get hit by a car, but there is no safe way to cross the street. It is a **risk** to cross the street to the playground. At the playground, there are broken swings, and trash is everywhere. A huge tree branch lies across the slide. There are no state and federal services. As a result, nobody is taking care of the playground.

R. G. Roth

Text Evidence

1 Sentence Structure Ⓐ Ⓒ Ⓣ

Reread the fourth sentence in the second paragraph. Circle the comma. Draw a box around the part of the sentence that tells why you can have cookies for breakfast.

2 Specific Vocabulary Ⓐ Ⓒ Ⓣ

Reread the fifth sentence in the third paragraph. The word *risk* means "the possibility that something dangerous or bad might happen."

Why is it a risk to cross the street to the playground?

It is a risk because _____

_____.

3 Comprehension

Cause and Effect

Reread the third paragraph. Circle two things that happen when nobody is taking care of the playground.

1 **Comprehension**

Cause and Effect

Reread the first paragraph. Underline the words that tell what happens when the government does not maintain the parks.

2 **Sentence Structure** (A C T)

Reread the fifth sentence in the first paragraph. Circle the word that connects the two parts of the sentence. Then draw a box around the two parts of the sentence that can stand alone.

3 **Specific Vocabulary** (A C T)

Reread the last sentence in the first paragraph. The word *polluted* means "dangerously dirty." Underline what is polluted in the sentence.

Think about other things you love to do. Do you want to go to the beach? There are no lifeguards to keep you safe. Do you want to play soccer in the park? The state and local governments do not **maintain** the parks, so you will never find a safe place to play. Do you want to eat lunch outside? The air is too **polluted**.

Have you ever thought about how our country is protected? Remember, the government runs the army. Without the government, there is no army to protect us.

Back to the Real World

It is good we live in a world with rules. We live in a democracy. We have the right to vote for the people we want to run the country. The people we **elect** pass laws to help protect us. If a law needs to be changed, the government can pass an amendment to the law. Community workers such as police officers and lifeguards work to keep us safe. Government agencies like the Environmental Protection Agency **inspect** the air and water. It makes sure the air and water are clean.

Our government has laws, or rules, to keep us safe. The laws make sure everyone is treated fairly. Without rules, the world would be a different place.

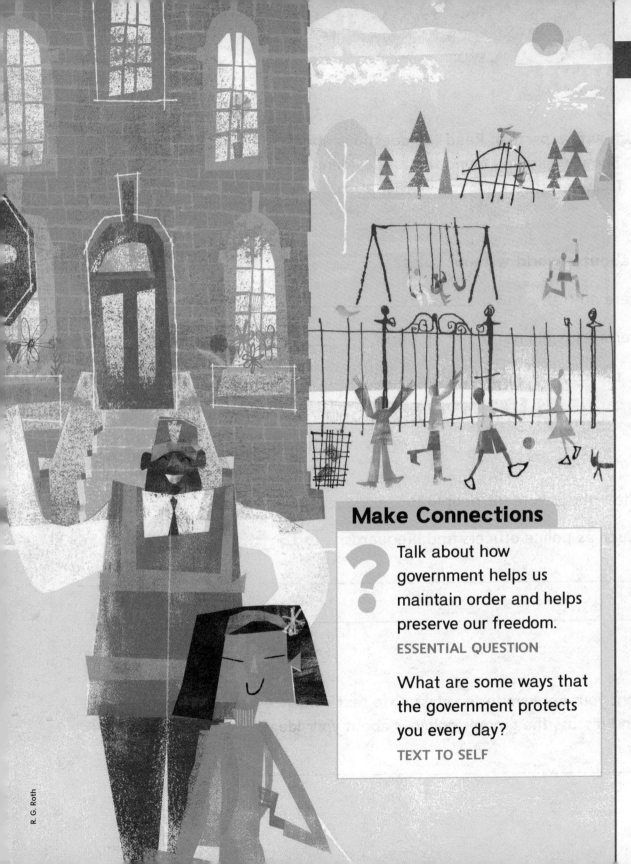

R. G. Roth

Make Connections

? Talk about how government helps us maintain order and helps preserve our freedom.
ESSENTIAL QUESTION

What are some ways that the government protects you every day?
TEXT TO SELF

 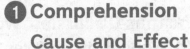
1 Comprehension
Cause and Effect

Reread the third paragraph on page 10. Underline the words that describe how the Environmental Protection Agency helps us.

2 Specific Vocabulary 🅰🅒🆃

Find the word *elect* in the third paragraph on page 10. *Elect* means "to choose someone by voting." Underline the part of the sentence that tells what the people elected do.

COLLABORATE

3 Talk About It

Reread the third paragraph. Discuss how democracy works. In a democracy we have the right to _____.

The people we elect pass laws to _____.

11

COLLABORATE

Partner Discussion Work with a partner. Read the questions about "A World Without Rules." Show where you found the text evidence. Write the page numbers. Then describe what you learned.

What did you learn about a world without rules?

I read that if there were no traffic laws, _____.

If state and local governments did not maintain parks, _____.

If there was no army, our country _____.

Text Evidence 🔍

Page(s): _____

Page(s): _____

Page(s): _____

How do rules help protect us?

I read that we have the right to vote for people to _____.

Community workers, such as police officers and lifeguards,

help to _____.

Laws help to _____.

Text Evidence 🔍

Page(s): _____

Page(s): _____

Page(s): _____

COLLABORATE

Group Discussion Present your answers to the class. Cite text evidence for your ideas. Listen to and discuss the group's opinions about your ideas.

I think your idea is _____.

Write Work with a partner. Look at your notes about "A World Without Rules." Then write your answer to the essential question. Use text evidence to support your answer. Use vocabulary words in your writing.

Why is government needed in a community?

The government makes sure that _____
_____.

Traffic laws help to _____
_____.

State and local governments help to maintain _____
_____.

Our government laws help to _____
_____.

Share Writing Present your writing to the class. Then talk about their opinions. Think about their ideas. Explain why you agree or disagree with their ideas. You can say:

I agree with _____.

I do not agree because _____.

13

Write to Sources

Take Notes About the Text I took notes on an idea web to answer the question: *Did the author do a good job of showing why we need government and rules?*

pages 8–11

Malia

Detail
Takes care of playgrounds and parks to keep them clean and safe.

Detail
Traffic laws keep us safe.

Main Idea
Why we need government and rules.

Detail
Government runs the army to protect our country.

Detail
Environmental Protection Agency keeps air and water clean and safe.

14

Write About the Text I used my notes from my idea web to write an opinion.

Student Model: *Opinion*

I think the author did a good job in showing why we need government and rules. We need traffic laws to stay safe. We need the government to take care of our playgrounds and parks. The Environmental Protection Agency makes sure the air and water are clean and safe. The government runs the army to protect our country. These reasons show why government and rules are very important.

TALK ABOUT IT

COLLABORATE

Text Evidence

Draw a box around a sentence that comes from the notes. Does the sentence provide a supporting detail?

Grammar

Circle the verbs. Why did Malia use this tense?

Condense Ideas

Underline the second and third sentences. How can you condense the sentences into one detailed sentence?

Your Turn

COLLABORATE

What was the best reason the author gave for why we need rules? Use text evidence.

>> *Go Digital*
Write your response online. Use your editing checklist.

TALK ABOUT IT

Weekly Concept Leadership

? **Essential Question**
Why do people run for public office?

>> *Go Digital*

COLLABORATE **Describe what the group in the photo is doing. The leaders of the group are marching in front. What are the qualities of a good leader? Write the words in the chart.**

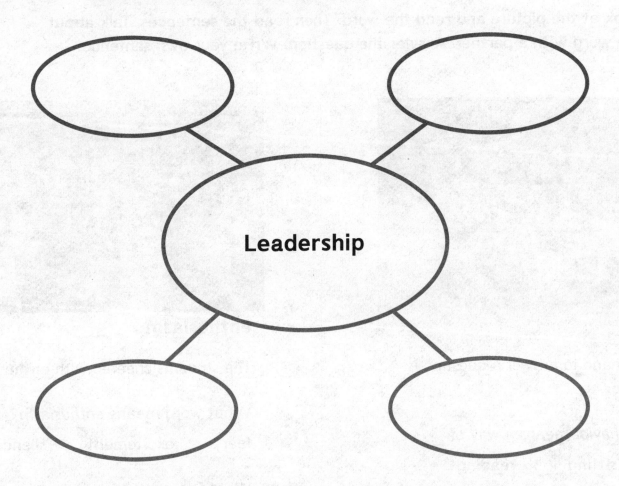

Leadership

Discuss why groups need leaders. Why do people become leaders? Use the words from the chart. You can say:

Groups need leaders who are _____.

A good leader wants to help others by _____.

COLLABORATE

Look at the picture and read the word. Then read the sentences. Talk about the word with a partner. Answer the question. Write your own sentence.

behavior

Raising your hand to answer a question is good **behavior**.

The word *behavior* means a way of

acting   **sitting**   **reading**

What is good behavior in school?

Good behavior in school is _____

_____.

enthusiasm

The students cheered with **enthusiasm**.

What word means *enthusiasm?*

fear   **excitement**   **silence**

What is something you have enthusiasm for at school?

I have enthusiasm for _____

_____.

Words and Phrases: Suffixes *-ful* and *-less*

The suffix *–ful* means "full of."

care**ful** = full of care

Who is careful crossing the street?

The family is **careful** crossing the street.

The suffix *–less* means "without."

tooth**less** = without teeth

Who is toothless?

The baby is **toothless**.

COLLABORATE

Talk with a partner. Look at the pictures. Read the sentences. Circle the meaning of the underlined word.

The fireworks are <u>colorful</u>.
  full of color   without color

The sky is <u>cloudless</u>.
  full of clouds   without clouds

COLLABORATE

1 Talk About It

Look at the picture. Read the title. Discuss what you see. Use these words.

glasses   monument   class

Write about what you see.

The boy is wearing special _____

_____.

Who is the boy with?

The boy is with _____

_____.

Where is the boy?

The boy is in front of a _____

_____.

Take notes as you read the story.

The TimeSpecs 3000

Essential Question

? **Why do people run for public office?**

Read how Miguel decides to run for class president.

20

September 15

Dear Grandpa,

I am home from our class trip to Washington, D.C., and I have a lot to tell you. I am going to run for class president!

Your invention, the TimeSpecs 3000, was very helpful. I got some good advice. I intend to tell you everything when I visit, but for now I have added my field notes to this e-mail.

FIELD NOTES: **DAY 1**

I use the TimeSpecs 3000 at the Washington **Monument**. A guide accompanies our class, and I put on the specs while she talks.

Immediately, I see the monument in the past. I watch the builders lay the first stone in 1848, and everybody's wearing funny hats and old-fashioned clothes. When I take off the TimeSpecs 3000, I am back in the present. My class is going to lunch.

Chris Boyd

Text Evidence

1 Sentence Structure ⒶⒸⓉ

Reread the first sentence in the first paragraph. Circle the word that connects the two parts of the sentence. Underline the two parts of the sentence that can stand on their own.

2 Specific Vocabulary ⒶⒸⓉ

Reread the first sentence in the third paragraph. The word *monument* can be "a building or statue that was built to remind people of an important person or event." Underline who this monument was built for.

COLLABORATE

3 Talk About It

Describe what happens when Miguel puts on the TimeSpecs 3000.

He sees the monument _____.

People are wearing _____

_____.

21

1 Specific Vocabulary Ⓐ Ⓒ Ⓣ

Look at the fourth sentence in the first paragraph. The word *immature* means "not acting the correct way." Underline the sentence that describes why the classmates are immature.

2 Sentence Structure Ⓐ Ⓒ Ⓣ

Look at the fourth sentence in the second paragraph. Circle the punctuation marks that show someone is speaking. Who is speaking to Miguel? Draw a box around the words that tells you who is speaking.

COLLABORATE

3 Talk About It

Describe the advice Lincoln's statue gives Miguel.

First you can run for _____.

When you get used to being

_____, you can run for

_____.

FIELD NOTES: **DAY 2**

We are back on the National Mall. It is not like the mall at home. This mall is outside and has a reflecting pool. The **behavior** of my classmates is **immature**. They are running around and throwing pebbles in the pool. I want to learn about history on my own, so I put on the TimeSpecs 3000 and look at the Lincoln Memorial.

Lincoln's statue is amazing. I want to help people like he did. I think about running for class president. Suddenly, a voice says, "Are you running for president?" I look up and realize the statue is talking to me. I was speechless.

The statue says, "Maybe you can first run for mayor of your town. When you get used to being mayor, you can run for president."

I say, "Actually, I want to be president of my class."

The statue nods. "That's a good start."

I decide to tell Lincoln about my problem. "I hate writing and giving speeches. And my opponent, Tommy, is great at both things."

"What are your campaign ideas?" Lincoln asks.

I tell him, "I have lots of ideas for our school. I want our school cafeteria to buy fruits and vegetables from the farmer's market. I also want to start a book drive for our school library."

"There's your speech," Lincoln says. "Tell people your ideas with honesty and **enthusiasm**, and they will listen."

I say, "Thanks, Mr. President. "I think I can do that!"

Grandpa, I can't wait to see you on Saturday. I want to tell you about our trip to the Natural History Museum.

Your grandson and future class president,

Miguel.

P.S. It isn't a good idea to wear TimeSpecs 3000 looking at dinosaur bones!

Make Connections

? Talk about why Miguel decides to run for class president. **ESSENTIAL QUESTION**

What would you do for your school if you were class president? **TEXT TO SELF**

Chris Boyd

1 Comprehension
Point of View

Reread the first paragraph. What is Miguel's point of view of his opponent? Underline the sentence that tells you.

2 Sentence Structure Ⓐ Ⓒ Ⓣ

Reread the second sentence in the fourth paragraph. Underline the word that connects the two parts of the sentence. Circle who the pronoun *they* refers to.

COLLABORATE

3 Talk About It

Discuss Miguel's ideas for the school if he becomes president.

He wants the school to _____

_____.

He also wants to start _____

_____.

Respond to the Text

Partner Discussion Work with a partner. Read the questions about "The TimeSpecs 3000." Show where you found the text evidence. Write the page numbers. Then discuss what you learned.

What does Miguel learn in Washington, D.C.?

Text Evidence 🔍

When Miguel uses the TimeSpecs 3000 at the Washington

Monument, he sees _____. 　　Page(s): _____

Miguel says he wants to run for _____. 　　Page(s): _____

Some of Miguel's campaign ideas are _____. 　　Page(s): _____

What advice does Lincoln's statue give Miguel?

Text Evidence 🔍

President Lincoln tells Miguel to start by _____. 　　Page(s): _____

President Lincoln tells Miguel to tell people his ideas with _____ 　　Page(s): _____

and _____.

Group Discussion Present your answers to the class. Cite text evidence for your ideas. Listen to and discuss the group's opinions about your ideas.

I think your idea is _____.

COLLABORATE

Write Work with a partner. Look at your notes about "The TimeSpecs 3000." Then write your answer to the essential question. Use text evidence to support your answer. Use vocabulary words in your writing.

Why does Miguel want to run for class president?

Miguel decides to run for class president after Lincoln's statue tells him

_____

_____ .

Miguel's ideas for helping the school are _____

_____ .

COLLABORATE

Share Writing Present your writing to the class. Then talk about their opinions. Talk about their ideas. Explain why you agree or disagree with their ideas. You can say:

I agree with _____ .

I do not agree because _____ .

Write to Sources

pages 20–23

Take Notes About the Text I took notes on this idea web about the story to help me respond to this prompt: *Write an email from Miguel to his grandfather. Have Miguel tell what he saw when he put on the TimeSpecs 3000 at the dinosaur bones.*

Ricky

What happened when Miguel put on TimeSpecs 3000 in Washington, D.C.?

Saw the Washington Monument in 1848.

Lincoln's statue started talking to him.

Lincoln gave advice about running for class president.

Write About the Text I used the notes from my idea web to write an email from Miguel to his grandfather about what happened when he looked at the dinosaur bones with the TimeSpecs 3000.

Student Model: *Narrative Text*

Dear Grandpa,

     Our class visited the Natural History Museum. I liked seeing the Washington Monument in 1848. So I put on the TimeSpecs 3000 in front of some dinosaur bones. Then a very big dinosaur flew down in front of me. I felt its hot breath on my face. I was afraid it was going to have me for dinner. So I took off the TimeSpecs 3000. Then, I was back with the old dinosaur bones.

Love,

Miguel

TALK ABOUT IT

Text Evidence
Draw a box around a detail that comes from the notes. Why is this detail important?

Grammar
Circle the pronouns *I* and *me*. Who does *each pronoun refer to*?

Connect Ideas
Underline the second and third sentences. How can you make the sentences into one sentence?

Your Turn

Write an email from Miguel to President Lincoln. Have Miguel tell how he felt when he gave his speech for class president.

>> *Go Digital*
Write your response online. Use your editing checklist.

TALK ABOUT IT

?

Essential Question

How do inventions and technology affect your life?

>> Go Digital

COLLABORATE

Look at the photo. Describe what you see. How can technology make a person's life better? Write words in the chart.

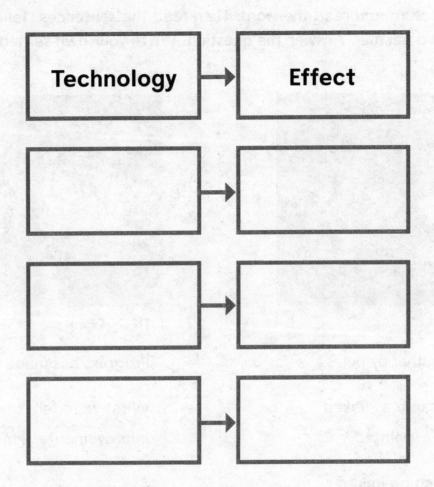

Technology	→	Effect
	→	
	→	
	→	

Discuss how technology can change people's lives. Use the words from the chart. You can say:

The technology of _____ can help people.

It helps people _____.

More Vocabulary

COLLABORATE

Look at the picture and read the word. Then read the sentences. Talk about the word with a partner. Answer the question. Write your own sentence.

linked

The wires are **linked** together by poles.

What word means the same as *linked?*

used   joined   painted

What are things that can be linked together?

Things that can be linked together are _____

_____

_____.

progress

Progress has made phones better.

What word tells the meaning of *progress?*

improvement   kindness   statement

Progress happens when things are _____

_____

_____.

Words and Phrases: *behind* and *outside*

The word *behind* means "at the back of."

Where is the donkey?

The donkey is **behind** the fence.

The word *outside* means "in the open air."

Where are the children racing?

The children are racing **outside**.

 Talk with a partner. Look at the pictures. Read the sentences.
Write the word that completes the sentence.

The ducklings are swimming _____ their mother.

    behind outside

They are doing their homework _____.

    behind outside

COLLABORATE

1 Talk About It

Look at the picture. Read the title. Discuss what you see. Use these words.

poles   wires   man   girl

Write about what you see.

I see _____

_____

_____.

What are the man and girl doing?

The man and the girl are _____

_____

_____.

Take notes as you read the story.

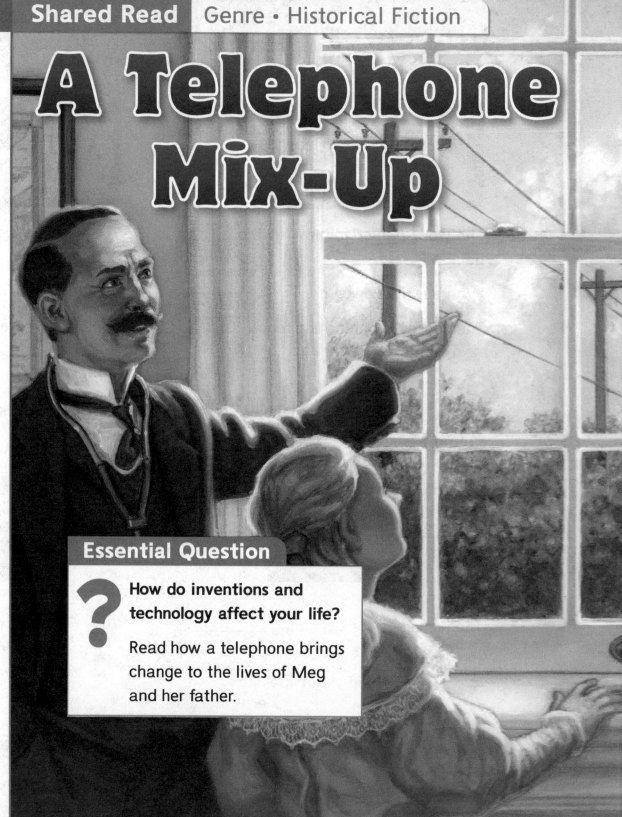

A Telephone Mix-Up

Essential Question

?

How do inventions and technology affect your life?

Read how a telephone brings change to the lives of Meg and her father.

32

Dr. Ericksen said to his daughter, Meg, "By tomorrow afternoon there will be eight telephones here in Centerburg, Ohio. And one of them will be in our home! I predict that before this decade is over, there will be a hundred telephones in town! When people need help, they will call me on the telephone. Think about how many lives this technology will save!"

Meg knew that many people did not think telephones were a good idea. They said that telephones were a **useless** invention. Others said the new machines will cause problems. People will stop visiting each other and stop writing letters.

But that did not stop **progress**. The town's first telephone was set up in the general store, and another was put in the hotel. Mrs. Kane was the town's first switchboard operator. She connected the calls coming in to the correct lines.

The next morning, on October 9, 1905, Meg was in class. She was thinking about what life will be like with a phone in the house. Then she was wishing for the long school day to end.

 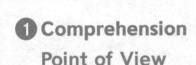

❶ Comprehension

Point of View

Reread the first paragraph. The author thinks telephones will be helpful. Underline one sentence that shows why the author thinks telephones will be helpful.

❷ Specific Vocabulary Ⓐ Ⓒ Ⓣ

Look at the word *useless* in the second paragraph. The suffix *-less* means "not having."

What is the meaning of useless?

_____

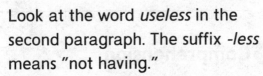

Underline what people think is useless.

❸ Sentence Structure Ⓐ Ⓒ Ⓣ

Reread the last paragraph. Who does the pronoun *she* refer to? Circle the person's name. Underline why she was wishing for the long school day to end.

33

Text Evidence

COLLABORATE

1 Talk About It

Reread the first paragraph. Discuss why Meg is excited to see the wood poles and wires.

Meg is excited because she

imagines _____

_____.

2 Comprehension

Point of View

Reread the second paragraph. What is the author's point of view about the new telephone? Underline the words that tell you.

3 Sentence Structure **A C T**

Reread the second and third sentences in the sixth paragraph. Combine the two sentences into one sentence. Rewrite the sentence.

_____

_____

_____.

34

On the walk home, Meg looked at the tall wood poles. Thick wires **linked** one pole to another, and Meg imagined each wire carrying the words of friends. She thought about people sharing news and birthday wishes.

Meg ran into the house, letting the door slam shut behind her. On the wall was the gleaming wood telephone box with its black receiver on a hook. Her father smiled and asked, "Have you ever seen such magnificence?"

Suddenly the telephone rang, and they both jumped.

Her father picked up the receiver and shouted, "Hello, yes, this is the doctor! Mrs. Kane, there is too much static. I can't hear you. Did you say Turner farm?"

As her father hung up the phone, Meg asked, "Can I go with you, Father?"

"Yes, let's go," her father said. He grabbed his medical bag. And they went outside to the horse and carriage.

When they got to the farm they saw Mr. Turner walking to the barn.

Dr. Ericksen said, "Jake, I got here as fast as I could. Is Mrs. Turner sick?"

Jake Turner looked **confused**, but he took them to the barn.

In the barn was a baby goat and its mother. The baby snorted and looked unhappy.

Dr. Ericksen said, "Jake, I'm no vet! You need Dr. Kerrigan."

"I wondered why you showed up. I guess there was a mix-up," Jake said.

Dr. Ericksen laughed and said, "I'll send for Dr. Kerrigan when I get back."

The telephone was very useful to the town, but sometimes there were mix-ups. Meg and her father called a mix-up "another sick goat."

Make Connections

? How did the invention of the telephone affect the town of Centerburg? ESSENTIAL QUESTION

Think of an invention and tell how it has affected your life. TEXT TO SELF

1 Sentence Structure Ⓐ Ⓒ Ⓣ

Reread the first paragraph. Circle the punctuation marks that show someone is speaking. Underline who Dr. Ericksen thinks is sick.

2 Specific Vocabulary Ⓐ Ⓒ Ⓣ

Reread the second paragraph. The word *confused* means "did not understand or think clearly." Why was Jake confused?

Jake was confused because

_____

_____.

COLLABORATE

3 Talk About It

Discuss what happened when Meg and her father arrived at the Turner farm.

Jake took them to the _____.

They saw a _____

_____.

35

Tristan Elwell

Respond to the Text

Partner Discussion Work with a partner. Read the questions about "A Telephone Mix-Up." Show where you found the text evidence. Write the page numbers. Then describe what you learned.

COLLABORATE

How did people feel about telephones when they came to Centerburg?

Text Evidence 🔍

Dr. Ericksen thought the telephone _____.

Page(s): _____

Other people thought the telephone would cause problems because

_____.

Page(s): _____

Meg imagined the telephone wires carried _____.

Page(s): _____

What happened on the first afternoon that the Ericksens had a telephone?

Text Evidence 🔍

Dr. Ericksen received a call asking _____.

Page(s): _____

Dr. Ericksen and Meg went to the Turner farm, but _____.

Page(s): _____

Dr. Ericksen said he will send for _____ when he gets back.

Page(s): _____

Group Discussion Present your answers to the class. Cite text evidence for your ideas. Listen to and discuss the group's opinions about your ideas.

COLLABORATE

I think your idea is _____.

Write Work with a partner. Look at your notes about "A Telephone Mix-Up." Then write your answer to the essential question. Use text evidence to support your answer. Use vocabulary words in your writing.

COLLABORATE

How did inventions and technology affect the Ericksens?

The Ericksens received one of the first telephones in _____

_____.

Dr. Ericksen thinks the telephone will help _____

_____.

At the end of the story, the Ericksens learned the telephone can be useful, but _____

_____.

Share Writing Present your writing to the class. Then talk about their opinions. Talk about their ideas. Explain why you agree or disagree with their ideas. You can say:

COLLABORATE

I agree with _____.

I do not agree because _____.

Write to Sources

pages 32–35

Patrice

Take Notes About the Text I took notes on the sequence chart about the story. It will help me to respond to the prompt: *Write a dialogue between Meg and her father. Have them talk about what happened at the Turner farm.*

Meg and her father, Dr. Ericksen, get a new phone.

Dr. Ericksen gets a call. It is hard to hear what the caller is saying. They go to the Turner farm.

Meg and her father go to the farm. The Turners have a sick goat. They need a vet.

Meg and her father call telephone mix-ups "another sick goat."

38

Write About the Text I used the notes from my chart to write a dialogue between Meg and her father about what happened on the Turner farm.

Student Model: *Narrative Text*

Meg said, "Father, that was a big mix up at the Turner's farm today."

"Yes, it was. They needed a vet, not a doctor. Next time I will ask more questions. I will ask for more details before we go," her father said.

"Good idea!" Meg said. "We don't want 'another sick goat.'"

TALK ABOUT IT

Text Evidence
Draw a box around a detail from the notes. Why is this detail important for the dialogue?

Grammar
Circle an example of the future tense. Why does Patrice use the future tense here?

Condense Ideas
Underline the two sentences that tell about what Meg's father will do the next time. How can you make these sentences into one detailed sentence?

Your Turn

Write a dialogue between Dr. Ericksen and Dr. Kerrigan about the telephone mix-up. Use text evidence.

>> Go Digital
Write your response online. Use your editing checklist.

?

Essential Question

How do you explain what you
see in the sky?

>> *Go Digital*

COLLABORATE

Look at the photo. Describe what you see. What things do you see in the sky at night? Write the words in the chart.

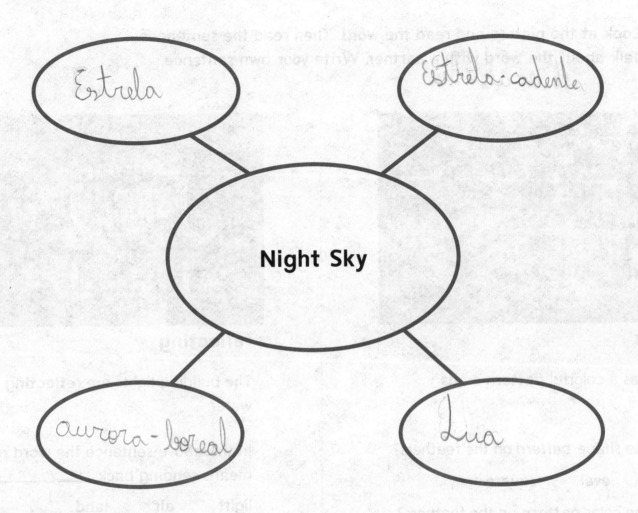

Estrela

Estrela-cadente

Night Sky

aurora-boreal

Lua

Discuss what you can see in the sky at night. Use the words from the chart. You can say:

I can see the _aurora-boreal_ in the night sky.

I can also see the _Estrela_ in the night sky.

COLLABORATE

Look at the picture and read the word. Then read the sentences.
Talk about the word with a partner. Write your own sentence.

patterns

The bird has a colorful **pattern** on its feathers.

What is the shape *pattern* on the feathers?

triangle   **oval**   **square**

What is the color **pattern** on the feathers?

The color pattern is _____

_____.

reflecting

The building lights are **reflecting** off the water.

In the above sentence the word *reflecting* means sending back _____.

light   **air**   **land**

What other things can you see lights reflect off of?

I can see lights *reflect* off _____

_____.

Words and Phrases: Suffixes *-ion* and *-ness*

The suffix *-ion* means "the act of." Adding *-ion* to a verb will change the word into a noun.

direct + *-ion* = direction

The sign tells you which **direction** to go.

The suffix *-ness* means "the state or condition of."

kind + *-ness* = the state of being kind

The woman shows her **kindness** by helping the man.

Talk with a partner. Look at the pictures. Read the sentences. Add an ending to the underlined word to complete the sentence.

They look at the map to find the right <u>direct</u> _____.

           -ion   -ness

She shows <u>kind</u> _____ to the dog.

           -ion   -ness

COLLABORATE

❶ Talk About It

Look at the photograph. Read the title. Discuss what you see. Use these words.

sky   lights   night

Write about what you see.

I see _lights in the ninght sky._

What does the sky look like?

The sky is filled with _many colors and gas._

Take notes as you read the text.

Wonders of the Night Sky

Essential Question

? How do you explain what you see in the sky?

Read about what causes some of the sights you see in the sky.

somenthing that repeats

Day becomes night (as) Earth turns on its axis. At night, you may see many different kinds of light. You may see one of the phases of the moon. Or you may see **patterns** of colored lights spread across the sky. People love to look at the night sky. And scientists try to explain what we see.

The Northern Lights

The northern lights are an amazing light show. It is also called "aurora borealis." Every few years, they can be seen in the skies near the North Pole. Bright stripes of green, yellow, red, and blue lights appear in the sky.

People used to believe the lights were caused by sunlight **reflecting** off ice. They thought light bounced back from the ice and made patterns in the sky. But in fact, the lights happen because of Earth's magnetic field.

The sun gives off electric **particles** that go in every direction. These particles join together in a stream, called a solar wind. When the solar winds reach Earth's magnetic field, strong electric charges occur. These electric charges cause the colorful lights in the sky.

The northern lights above Hammerfest, Norway

Picture Press/Alamy

1 Sentence Structure A C T

Reread the first sentence in the first paragraph. Circle the word *as*. It tells about two things that are happening at the same time. Underline the two things.

2 Specific Vocabulary A C T

Reread the first sentence in the fourth paragraph. The word *particles* means "tiny pieces of matter." Underline the kind of particles the sun gives off.

What happens to the particles the sun gives off?

The particles the sun gives off

Eletrical

3 Comprehension
Cause and Effect

Reread the fourth paragraph. Circle the words that tell what causes the colorful lights in the sky.

45

Text Evidence

COLLABORATE

① Talk About It

Discuss why long ago people were afraid of comets.

Long ago, people were afraid of comets because _they linghts brought war and sikness._

② Sentence Structure Ⓐ Ⓒ Ⓣ

Reread the first sentence in the second paragraph. Circle the commas. Underline the words that tell what comets are made of.

③ Comprehension
Cause and Effect

Reread the second paragraph. Underline the sentence that tells what causes the tail of the comet.

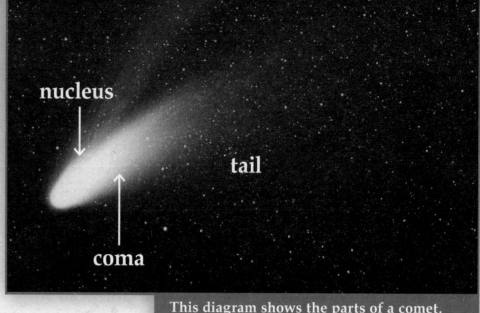

nucleus

tail

coma

This diagram shows the parts of a comet. Some comets' tails can be very long.

Comets

Another kind of light that moves across the night sky is a comet. The word *comet* comes from a Greek word. It means "wearing long hair." Long ago, people thought comets looked like stars with long hair. They were afraid of the strange lights and thought the lights brought war and sickness.

Today we know comets are made of rock, dust, ice, and frozen gases. A comet moves around the sun. When the comet comes close to the sun, a "tail" of gas and dust is pushed out behind the comet. This long tail is what we see from Earth.

Scientists think comets are some of the oldest objects in space. They watch certain comets and can predict when we can see them from Earth.

Meteors

Some nights you may see shooting stars. Shooting stars are not really stars. They are meteors. Meteors are the rocky pieces of debris that enter Earth's atmosphere. Sometimes Earth passes through an area in space with a lot of debris. This is when a meteor shower occurs. You may see hundreds of "shooting stars" on the night of a meteor shower.

The Perseid meteor shower

Anyone with a telescope can learn about space. Look up at the night sky and you will see amazing things.

Make Connections

? Talk about what causes some of the sights in the night sky. ESSENTIAL QUESTION

What do you wonder about when you look up at the night sky? TEXT TO SELF

Text Evidence

1 Comprehension

Cause and Effect

Reread the first paragraph. Underline the word that tells what shooting stars are. Then circle the sentence that tells what causes shooting stars.

2 Sentence Structure **A C T**

Reread the second and third sentences in the first paragraph. Underline the words that can replace the pronoun *they*.

3 Specific Vocabulary **A C T**

Reread the fourth sentence in the first paragraph. The word *debris* means "pieces of something that is left after it has been destroyed." Circle what meteors are made up of.

Respond to the Text

Partner Discussion Work with a partner. Read the questions about "Wonders of the Night Sky." Show where you found the text evidence. Write the page numbers. Then describe what you learned.

COLLABORATE

What did I learn about the northern lights?

Long ago people believed the northern lights were caused by _nucleus-_ _____ that the ____ by a neoron tron- ____ northern light _____.

Text Evidence 🔍

Page(s): _____

Today, scientists know the northern lights are caused by _because_ gas en northorn linghts _____.

Page(s): _____

What did I learn about comets and meteors?

Comets are made of _____, _____, _____, and _____.

When a comet comes close to the sun, it causes a _____.

Meteors are rocky pieces of debris that _____.

Text Evidence 🔍

Page(s): _____

Page(s): _____

Page(s): _____

Group Discussion Present your answers to the class. Cite text evidence for your ideas. Listen to and discuss the group's opinions about your ideas.

COLLABORATE

I think your idea is _____.

Write Work with a partner. Look at your notes about "Wonders of the Night Sky." Then write your answer to the essential question. Use text evidence to support your answer. Use vocabulary words in your writing.

How do scientists explain what we see in the night sky?

The northern lights are caused by _____

_____.

As a comet moves around the sun, a _____

_____.

Meteors look like _____ but they are really _____

_____.

Share Writing Present your writing to the class. Then talk about their opinions. Think about their ideas. Explain why you agree or disagree with their ideas. You can say:

I agree with _____.

I do not agree because _____.

Write to Sources

pages 44–47

Take Notes About the Text I took notes on the idea web to answer the question: *What information does the author tell about what causes the northern lights?*

Jason

Detail
They happen because of Earth's magnetic field.

Detail
The sun gives off electric particles. They join together and become solar winds.

Main Idea
The information the author gives about the northern lights.

Detail
Solar winds reach Earth's magnetic field. It causes strong electric charges.

Detail
The electric charges cause the colorful lights.

Write About the Text I used my notes from my idea web to write a paragraph about the northern lights.

Student Model: *Informative Text*

The author tells about what causes the northern lights in "Wonders of the Night Sky." The northern lights happen because of Earth's magnetic field. The sun gives off electric particles. They join together and become solar winds. When solar winds reach the Earth's magnetic field, it causes electric charges. The electric charges cause the colorful lights of the northern lights in the sky. It is an amazing light show.

TALK ABOUT IT

Text Evidence

Draw a box around a detail from the notes about the northern lights. Does the sentence provide a supporting detail?

Grammar

Draw an arrow from the adjective *electric* to the noun it describes. Why was it important that Jason use the adjective *electric?*

Condense Ideas

Underline the two sentences that tell what causes the northern lights. How can you make the sentences into one detailed sentence using the word *which?*

Your Turn

What information does the author tell about comets? Use text evidence.

>> Go Digital
Write your response online. Use your editing checklist.

51

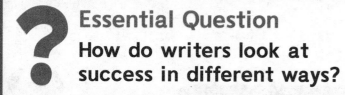

TALK ABOUT IT

? **Essential Question**
How do writers look at
success in different ways?

>> *Go Digital*

Describe what the boy in the photo is doing. Why does the writer use the photo to show success? Write the words in the chart.

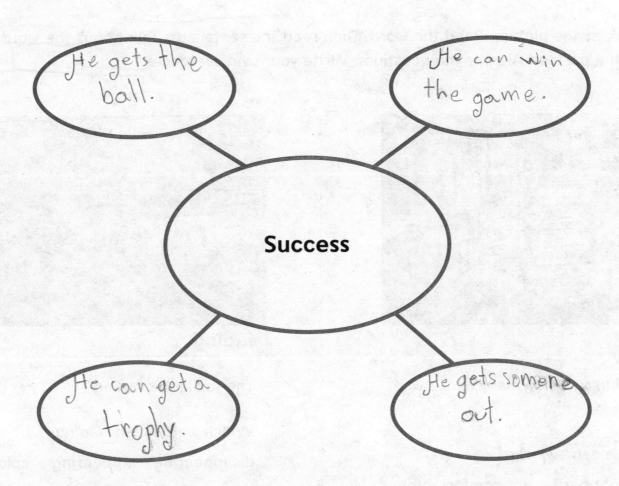

He gets the ball.

He can win the game.

Success

He can get a trophy.

He gets someone out.

Discuss different ways people show success. Use the words from the chart. You can say:

People show success when they _____.

They can also show success by _____.

More Vocabulary

COLLABORATE

Look at the picture. Read the word. Then read the sentences. Talk about the word with a partner. Answer the questions. Write your own sentences.

awkward

It is **awkward** to carry too many books at one time.

Which words mean *awkward*?

not heavy   not hard   not comfortable

What things can be awkward to carry?

It is awkward to carry _____

_____.

fading

The sunlight is **fading**.

Which word means *fading?*

disappearing   appearing   coloring

When does the sunlight start fading?

The sunlight starts fading _____

_____.

(l)zgr_pro/iStock/Getty Images Plus; (r)Commander John Bortniak - NOAA Corps - NOAA/Department of Commerce

54

Poetry Terms

stanza

A **stanza** is a group of two or more lines in a poem.
A stanza does not have to rhyme.

My sister and brother have fun running.
My sisters like jumping for fun.
I have fun watching them.

COLLABORATE

Work with a partner. Choose one phrase below. Use it two times. This makes repetition. Read your lines aloud to your partner.

go down   **fade away**

come up

I watch the sun

_____,

_____.

repetition

Repetition is repeating the same words or phrases in a poem.

The red and yellow balloon
floats away,
floats away.

❶ Literary Element

Stanza

A *stanza* is a group of lines in a poem. How many lines are in the first stanza?

_____

COLLABORATE

❷ Talk About It

Look at the boy. Discuss what you see. Reread the second stanza. Circle the words that describe what he is doing. Write the words.

_____

_____

❸ Specific Vocabulary Ⓐ Ⓒ Ⓣ

Look at the second stanza. The word *melody* means "an arrangement of sounds that make up a tune." Circle the words that tell how the poet is trying to learn a melody.

Take notes as you read the poem.

Sing to Me

Essential Question

? How do writers look at success in different ways?

Read a poet's story of success.

The cool white keys stretched for miles.
How would my hands pull
and sort through the notes,
blending them into music?

I practiced
and practiced all day.
My fingers reaching for a **melody**
that hung dangling,
like an apple just out of reach.

I can't do this.
I can't do this.

The day ground on,
notes leaping hopefully into the air,
hovering briefly, only to crash,
an **awkward** jangle, a tangle of noise
before slowly **fading** away.

My mom found me, forehead on the keys.
She asked, "Would you like some help?
It took months for my hands to do what I wanted."
She sat down on the bench,
her slender fingers plucking notes
from the air.

I can do this.
I can do this.

She sat with me every night that week,
working my fingers until their efforts
made the keys sing to me, too.

— Will Meyers

Text Evidence

❶ Comprehension
Theme

The boy keeps trying to play the piano. The theme of the poem is he doesn't give up. Reread the second stanza. Circle a detail that helps you identify the theme.

❷ Literary Element
Repetition

Reread the third stanza. Circle the words that are repeated. What can't the boy do?

He can't _____.

COLLABORATE

❸ Talk About It

Reread the poem. Who helps the boy? Discuss your answer. Find the words that tell you. Underline the words.

The boy's _____ helped him

learn to _____

_____.

Make Connections

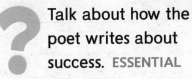

? Talk about how the poet writes about success. ESSENTIAL QUESTION

How do you feel when you are successful? TEXT TO SELF

Respond to the Text

COLLABORATE

Partner Discussion Work with a partner. Read the questions about "Sing to Me." Show where you found the text evidence. Write the line numbers. Then discuss what you learned.

What is the poem about?

The boy describes practicing _____.

In the third stanza, the boy feels _____.

In the sixth stanza, the boy feels _____.

Text Evidence 🔍

Line(s): _____

Line(s): _____

Line(s): _____

How does the boy succeed in the end?

In the beginning, the boy _____.

Then the boy's mother asks _____.

At the end of the poem, the boy _____.

Text Evidence 🔍

Line(s): _____

Line(s): _____

Line(s): _____

COLLABORATE

Group Discussion Present your answers to the class. Cite text evidence for your ideas. Listen to and discuss the group's opinions about your ideas.

I think your idea is _____.

Write Work with a partner. Look at your notes about "Sing to Me." Then write your answer to the essential question. Use text evidence to support your answer. Use vocabulary words in your writing.

How does the boy succeed in playing the piano?

In the beginning, the boy _____

_____

_____.

The boy gets help _____.

By the end of the poem, the boy _____

_____.

Share Writing Present your writing to the class. Then talk about their opinions. Talk about their ideas. Explain why you agree or disagree with their ideas. You can say:

I agree with _____.

I do not agree because _____.

Write to Sources

Alex

Take Notes About the Text I took notes on the chart to answer the question: *How does the poet of "Sing to Me" use repetition?*

pages 56-57

Repetition

I practiced and practiced all day.

I can't do this.
I can't do this.

I can do this.
I can do this.

Write About the Text I used notes from my chart to write about how the poet of "Sing to Me" uses repetition.

Student Model: *Informative Text*

Repetition is when a poet repeats a word or a phrase. The poet says "I practiced and practiced." The poet repeats the word *practiced* to show how hard he is trying. "I can't do this. I can't do this" is another example. It shows that the poet is upset. He still can't play the piano. Then he repeats the words, "I can do this. I can do this." The poet is happy. Repetition is a good way to tell how the poet feels.

TALK ABOUT IT

COLLABORATE

Text Evidence

Draw a box around a sentence that comes from the notes. How does the sentence tell you how the poet is feeling?

Grammar

Draw an arrow from the pronoun *I* in the second sentence to the word it refers to.

Connect Ideas

Circle the sentences that tell you the poet is upset and why he feels this way. How can you use the word *because* to connect the sentences?

Your Turn

COLLABORATE

Write about something you were successful at doing. Tell about how you felt. Use repetition in your writing.

>> Go Digital
Write your response online. Use your editing checklist.